The Resemblance *of* All Things

The Resemblance *of* All Things

BERNARD J. LURIE

Foreword by Fred Lurie

RESOURCE *Publications* · Eugene, Oregon

THE RESEMBLANCE OF ALL THINGS

Copyright © 2022 The Estate of Bernard J. Lurie. All rights reserved. Except for brief quotations in critical publications or reviews, no part of this book may be reproduced in any manner without prior written permission from the publisher. Write: Permissions, Wipf and Stock Publishers, 199 W. 8th Ave., Suite 3, Eugene, OR 97401.

Resource Publications
An Imprint of Wipf and Stock Publishers
199 W. 8th Ave., Suite 3
Eugene, OR 97401

www.wipfandstock.com

PAPERBACK ISBN: 978-1-6667-3745-5
HARDCOVER ISBN: 978-1-6667-9691-9
EBOOK ISBN: 978-1-6667-9692-6

MARCH 25, 2022 9:51 AM

CONTENTS

Part One	1
Part Two	14
Part Three	27
Part Four	40

FOREWORD

In 2017, while acting as administrator of my brother Bernie's estate, I received a bill for the annual rental on a safe deposit box. This was the first I knew of the box. On being able to open the box, I found the text of *Resemblance* printed out in the version that you now hold. I also found stamped confirmations of copyright applications for *Resemblance* that Bernie made in 1988, 1989, and 1990. On being able to access the hard drive of an old computer, I saw that Bernie continued to make some modifications to the poem up to the early 2000's. At the time of my visit to the bank, the banker assisting me said that Bernie had not opened the box for over four years.

    Bernie never spoke to me or anyone else about his own writing. This includes Bobbi Lurie, our sister, who is herself a published poet. Once, while at my home and discussing some matter, Bernie referred to a website and told me his password. It was "resemblance." He immediately recalled it, didn't say anything else in connection with the word, and there was nothing in his expression or manner to indicate that the word "resemblance" held any other significance for him.

    Bernie never got to enjoy a period of retirement from work. When I once asked him what he would like to do in retirement, he just said that there were a lot of books he wanted to read. The books that he already owned tell a lot about his interests, and their influence can be seen throughout *Resemblance*. Bernie had quite a collection of works on religion and philosophy. He owned different editions and commentaries on the Torah, Jewish Prophets and Writings, books of the Talmud, as well as the New Testament, the Texts of Taoism, and works on Buddhism. Notable among his books on philosophy were several copies of Spinoza's works, as well as scholarship and biographies of Spinoza. He had an anthology and some other volumes of contemporary poetry, including Bobbi's three books. The

Foreword

largest proportion of Bernie's library consisted of classic works of fiction and English poetry. His poetry books were primarily traditional classics from the seventeenth century through the Romantic Period.

Resemblance is the product of Bernie's efforts stretching over many years to artistically express his thoughts about God, ethics, and the nature of things. It is my hope that by publishing it here, readers will discover verses of meaning and beauty that reflect Bernie's participation in the traditions that meant so much to him — "And we, so loved, by love our more remembrance make!"

Fred Lurie

THE RESEMBLANCE *of* ALL THINGS

Part One

The voice to Job that spoke from out the whirlwind:

I.

My love is the desire that all things should exist,
And should exist in an abundance without bound
Of both the possible and the impossible,
And the conceivable and inconceivable -
Both all that is too wonderful for your belief,
And that is horrible beyond imagining -
Heavens and hells in infinite measures meted.

So do not say of evil, "Why must these things be?,"
Nor of the good things ask, "Why do they not exist?";
For all things are, and all that might be must occur;
And as all numbers all the other numbers join
In sets whose permutations never know an end,
So too each thing is joined to every other thing
In sets of endless permutations of events.

II.

1.

My love is not the love that angel hosts proclaimed
When I at first had gathered them within My mind
To know their plans for the creation of the world -
Which with the good would banish every evil thing,
And form each earth with joy and happiness alone;
They hailed their vision, and together sang with praise,
That paradise alone might fill the realms of being.

But yet the Adversary silent stood apart,
So that I asked from where he came, and why alone
He was not pleased that only good might come to be;
He said, "I come from the potentiality
Of all the things that might exist, where I have seen
That being must neither have a limit nor a bound,
But every world discovers worlds still yet beyond."

I therefore said, "The Adversary speaks My will
That might exist and does exist must be the same,
And all that might be must be as the things themselves;
Else God would not be God to make a lesser world,
And love not love that would deny a thing its being;
For love itself decrees that all things should exist,
No matter how much good and evil must then be."

2.

I said, "Even if nothingness remained alone,
And there was neither a creator nor a cause,
There yet would still exist potentiality
That all the things that might exist might come to be;
And this potential would exist in such detail
That none might tell, nor would there be, a difference
Between the things that might be and reality.

"For this potential is itself reality,
And it is nothing less and nothing else than that;
And as there may not be a good or evil thing
That in potentiality may not be found,
So all things must inevitably rise to be,
That every Job might come to see his day of birth,
And none might call that day a darkness or a void."

3.

"And all the things that seem so solid and so true,
And have, being caused, both their beginnings and their ends,
Are as a dream without a point of reference
That in the absence of a waking mind seems real;
And just as matter is but mainly empty space,
So all is as emptiness touching emptiness,
Within whose sleep each seems to each a solid thing.

"For I am the Maker who makes by not making;
And being needs no cause, but is because it might,
That none should say, 'What was before this world arose?',
Nor, 'Why does something, and not nothingness, exist?',
Nor, 'How did a first cause create these solid things?',
Nor, 'If that cause was first, then who created it?';
But all things altogether seamlessly arise."

4.

"Such is the law by which the wise may understand
How love decrees forgiveness and true brotherhood -
That each must overlook his sufferings and pains
By knowing that all such things must be if all things are,
And none more than another has the right to be;
But each thing owes its being to every other thing,
And all things must exist if any might at all.

"So if you would bear this great and terrible love,
And be as Me to know all good and evil things,
Look now upon that city in which all things are,
And gaze upon the world without a roof or bound;
Cast off all limits, though they seem as God in heaven;
For God cannot be God if seen with limits bound,
But I am truly God who always am beyond."

III.

1.

There is a country of the mind within whose midst
There lies a city, and there within that city
There is no time, nor movement, nor any motion
Of the seasons, but all is as calm and as still
As a work of sculpted art - this is the city
Whose peace is from before the foundings of the world,
And whose silence pours forth all the realms of being.

And these are the rooms and houses of the city -
Every room is a still and frozen universe,
And every house a history made up of rooms;
And from each room to room there is a hall that makes
A moving picture in which time appears to flow;
And from each house to house there is a street that makes
From every world to world and life to life rebirth.

And though it seem impossible that there should be
A still and frozen universe for every room,
And every permutation of a thing to thing,
And slightest change or movement of a particle,
And each infinitesimal energy and pulse,
The only instant all have ever known is now,
And not a one has ever answered, "What is time?"

For now is but that place where all that might must dwell -
The rooms that you remember, and that are to come,
The ancients and descendants, and the lives and worlds
And histories of every thing that was and will -
That not the smallest thing is ever truly lost,
But now is present somewhere within that city -
Where all exist as in a single moment's time.

2.

There is a house for every history that must be -
Both every house where science rules, and every house
Predestined as to that which in its times occurs;
And every combination of a room to room
That makes those halls whose doors, unopened, yet exist -
Where you have never lost your children nor your flocks,
Or where you know yet greater miseries than these.

There is a house for every hall that never ends
Until it makes once more the pasts of rooms once known -
Not just that histories eternally recur,
With endless repetition of each choice the same,
But that they might recur in many different ways
To let you choose again each instant that you lost,
Or thwart beforehand every circumstance of pain.

There is a house for every hall that seems to break
The laws of science, or other laws than yours obeys -
Where rooms are not as like the rooms that they succeed,
But where the passing animation of each hall
Makes moving pictures of miraculous events -
Of every permutation of your hates and fears,
And every paradise of happiness made flesh.

There is a house for each of the absurdities
That must exist if all the things that might be are -
Where doors and halls string rooms together without end,
So that they make immortal life, or where the rooms
Where you remember all that was your life and death
Succeed the rooms that show your last and dying breath,
So that they grant to you a resurrected life.

3.

Be then a prophet who can never but be true,
No matter if you speak of Adam and of Eve,
Of Noah and the flood, of Sinai and the law,
And all the signs and miracles that Moses wrought -
Every thing that comes to your imagination,
And all that you have dreamt or that you have believed,
And every thing that you are thinking now - it is!

And be a prophet of the rooms that bear the name,
"The pains of Job, which must exist if all things are";
And know that neither choice nor fate nor accident
Has caused your misery, nor brought you to these depths,
But free will and predestination both being true,
The doors that you have chose, which I by love foredain,
Leave yet unclosed those doors, unchosen, which remain.

And be a prophet of the wonders that might be -
That if the future seeks to travel to the stars,
There is a room where that already is achieved
Where now is every triumph of space and mind and time,
And all the doors and halls that lead from you to them;
And there can be no wish, nor problem, fear nor bound,
Whose answer, once being sought, is not within Me found.

And be a prophet who does not need know the cause
How times and worlds and laws with effort first arose,
Nor how all the complexities of life were made,
Nor how a man from nothingness might have evolved;
But rest in knowledge that the things that you have seen,
Or will yet see, exist because they might exist,
And all those things that might be are and must occur.

4.

Then shall you, prophet, prove what cannot be disproved -
That if all things exist, there must exist each world
Where some things only, and not all things, seem to be,
And every you who sees the things that you perceive;
But there can be no worlds that might surpass all things,
Or that with certainty could say My love is not,
Or that there might not be a thing beyond their bounds.

For science is but a province within the empire
Of imagination, and never will explain
Why worlds exist in one way, and not other ways,
Nor ultimately why but some things only are;
But in the city there must be sufficient rooms
To make each law of science, and every change decreed
Between an instant and its each succeeding ones.

As other selves exist, though you know but your own,
So other worlds exist, though you know this alone;
And though their chance seems one within a trillion ones,
Yet how impossible your world itself would seem
To one at first attempting to imagine it!;
And there must be a trillion times a trillion worlds,
And even more, in which all things must come to be.

IV.

1.

When I had gathered once again the angel hosts,
I showed Myself surpassing all infinities,
That they might know the one alone who knows no bound;
I said, "Though I am the totality of all,
Yet when the all is counted, and its endlessness
Itself comes to an end, I am still yet beyond;
For all is but My name, and not My very self!

"And this must be the final proof that I exist -
That I must be that one who am because I might -
The potential of all potentialities;
And though no thing can be outside that which is all,
Yet there must be a one who from beyond the all
Contains and sees that all, and its least detail knows -
Whose seeing is itself potentiality!

"As he who searches on a path without an end
Eventually must find the object of his quest,
So each inhuman space and mathematic void,
Though seeming an infinity, must be surpassed
Until transhumanized there is discovered one
Knowing knowledge unknowable but to Himself -
Who being all, must also be, yes, a person!"

2.

But yet the Adversary silent stood apart,
So that I asked, "Are you not pleased that all things are?";
He said, "Though every good and evil thing now is,
Yet You remain untouched by suffering and pain;
And how can all be all, and how can God be God,
If you too are not one whom that all must contain?;
Or each one thing be not, as much as all things, might?"

I therefore said, "The Adversary speaks My will
That My experience of each good and evil thing
Must also be among the things that might exist,
And I must know and feel the joys and pains of each -
That I who am the all must also be each part,
To make each part that all as much as all things are,
And My desire in each My love as much as love."

I said, "Each thing that harms a part must harm Myself,
That My desire must be that harm did not exist,
And all its cause extinguished into nothingness;
And in that nothingness is that which was at first -
Potentiality that all might come to be -
Which now that part must be which, suffering harm, was Me -
As it, though part, being Me, must, as all things, all be."

3.

"Such is the punishment of those who cause a harm -
Both all those harms each hates, and those that seem as good -
That they become the parts they harmed, and know their pains;
And endless are the nothingnesses born of harm -
Which each become a self that dreams experience -
That many are the cities, not just one alone,
And those who share each house - whose life each calls his own.

"So though all choices must eternally exist
Within the frozen rooms and halls of the cities,
Cursed are they who make the choice of wickedness,
And cursed most who choose the most or cruelest harms,
For greatest is the suffering they who choose must know,
Until by pain their harmlessness exceeds their harm,
And I desire no more that they were nothingness."

V.

1.

"What then is not extinguished, but must yet endure?;
But all those things whose joyfulness exceeds their harm,
And every thing that seems a harm, but truly helps,
And every righteousness that bears no harm at all -
The deeds by which one loves one's neighbor as oneself,
And does not do to others that which others hate,
But to those others does as wish it done oneself.

"So blessed is My sight, which makes the moral law,
That harms and joys, being seen, be in their balance judged -
The deeds and lives whose righteousness exceeds their harm,
That I might wish their house, in spite of all, might be;
And those who at the instant of their deeds endure,
Or who forgiving, are forgiven for their harms,
Or doing greatest deeds, endure the most of all."

2.

"Such is the creation of the newer city -
That I who know and feel the joys and pains of each,
Not wish alone that every cause of harm not be,
But all that is a joy, or cause of joy, desire -
That every righteous life and instant of a deed,
And all else that is not extinguished, but endures,
Might be as much as all that all which love has made.

"And that each love, though part, might fill each up the whole,
Each love with other love must mutually exist
In that one place that rightfully belongs to each -
Where joy for others joys, desires what they desire,
And every thing is made an omnipresent being
To share reality, and so communicate
With each thing, both the trivial and the most profound."

3.

"Within this newer city every place is one,
Each thing is every thing, and every part the whole;
Here every self is one, though each still yet exists,
And every mundane thing remains as once it was,
But is together joined with every space and time -
As if the heavens opened in the light of day,
Or dust and blood were resurrected to the skies.

"Here all things are as if they were but one alone;
And as a man is many parts that make a one,
Who stays a one though parts of him be sacrificed,
So here, though every cause of harm no longer be,
It is as all still were, for yet the one remains;
And thereby shows a greater love than was at first -
That each for every other sacrifices self."

VI.

1.

The angel hosts in unison proclaimed My love,
"What in us is wonder in God is accomplishment!;
For we are but the mirror of which You are the light;
And now we know the good of which we spoke at first
Was not the good that You have truly called Your own -
That he who searches far enough beyond each bound
Must always see Your love make yet a greater good!

"We see all that was not - a single moment's time;
And all that which is all - a moment that is now;
And all that shall be one - a moment yet-to-come;
And from these moments joined a greater time we see -
Which passes, not as time, from past to future things,
But from all that was less to greater things transpires;
Until what was but might, so pardoned, love desires!

"We see the nothingness as but a greater past;
And the cities we see as a greater present;
And the newer city as a greater future -
A world-to-come towards which all joys, unselfed, aspire;
But every harm extinguished back to nothingness
Must know again the world - the cities with their pains -
Where each those harms-that-were potential rise once more!

"We see the cities are to the greater future
A greater past that might, in so being past, be loved -
As all their hated things have in them passed away;
And though My love be satisfied that all things are,
And must be faced by those who, unforgiven, harm,
Yet mercy so with love a greater love unfolds -
That all their harms being past, they are as if no more!"

2.

"We see the moments as a serpent spiral on;
For yet the Adversary silent always comes
To show yet further moments and yet greater times,
And always greater realizations of Your name;
And he too is Your servant though we knew it not -
The one who always shows that You must be beyond -
Who does not praise though all the angel hosts shout, Hail!

"We see unfolding every newer greater being -
A greater all rising from the newer city,
And a greater newer city rising from that;
We see a yet greater all things rising from that,
And a yet greater newer city rise from that;
We see a still yet greater all things rise from that,
And a still yet greater newer city from that!

"We see the moments spiral onward and yet on -
All the moments frozen in a greater moment,
And greater moments making a yet greater time;
And all those greaters frozen in a yet greater;
And yet greaters making a still yet greater time;
And still yet greaters making even greater time;
And onward without bound, nor limit yet being found!"

VII.

See, Job, the final moment of the greatest time -
Where every tear of harm is finally wiped clean,
And even the Adversary joins in with praise -
And know the times but seemed required to those in bounds -
Whose sight of Me by future times must be surpassed;
For I have always been the one beyond all times -
The greatest moment in which every moment is!

As the book is read in time, but once it is read,
Is known in an instant; as the music is played
In time, but once finished, is complete in memory -
See Me who am what I am, who was what I was
And who always shall be what I always shall be;
And in that rest declare Me as the fast and still
Who all at once in one swift victory exists!

Part Two

The still small voice Elijah heard upon the mount:

I.

1.

My presence is the strange that some at some times know -
Which makes you think how strange it is to be at all -
That you should be this one whom others call yourself,
And share with every thing the being of this world!;
How strange the here where every thing that is exists -
That you should seem to be the only thing that is,
And all else merely the perceptions of your mind!

How strange the one alone that cannot be explained -
Which makes the mystery that this world should be a play,
And it be you who act the player of your part!;
How strange that though by nature all might come to pass
To make a world and self identical to yours,
They would but be a duplicate that would not know
That you, and not another, see the things you see!

2.

So go and tell My people not to seek for Me
Within the endless hierarchies of the great,
Nor in those gods the nations worship from below;
But seek Me as that one whom Abraham had sought -
Whom each thing may contain, but nothing can confine,
And who, though crowned the glorious Lord of hosts, would say,
"How strange that I should be so limited to this!"

For not by wonders, neither by a miracle,
Nor by the glories of a heaven am I known -
As those are things that, if the universe be vast,
Inevitably in the course of worlds must be;
But in that strange that equally in small and great
Makes highest heavens seem as trivial as the dust,
And dust as much the tabernacle of My name!

II.

My presence is the one before whom all shall stand
When at the end of times the final judgment comes,
And even this, the greatest moment, is surpassed;
Then all the angel hosts shall gather in My mind,
And with them too the Adversary shall appear,
That he might come as the accuser of the world,
And bring all things to that last great apocalypse.

And he shall say, "This greatest moment must now end,
And in its place another greatest moment rise -
As even boundless things but fill the realms they know -
Which seeing new dimensions, must then pass away;
And by their righteousness not one thing shall be saved,
Though they had earned the greatest cities as reward,
And all that must with all at this last judgment end.

"For You who are this greatest moment must now die,
And as the bubble of an instant disappear,
That You who also are the holiness beyond -
Who are that one alone that cannot be explained,
And separate from this greatest moment stands apart
And says, 'How strange and limited is even all!' -
Might sole remain when all this world shall pass away!"

But yet the angel hosts shall plead before My throne,
"Not You who stand apart from that which is the all,
And of Your own will sacrifice what You have been,
Shall as another rise, alone, a part of You;
But each who stands apart, made separate from some part -
Which equally with all must also be Yourself -
That they have known that strange that You have known beyond!"

And I shall say, "The angel hosts proclaim My will
That every one who by a doubt, however small,
Has stood apart from self to know how strange he was,
And every thing that consecrated has been made
An object that in holiness has stood apart,
Shall be a portion of Myself who am beyond,
And as another from My seeming death shall rise!"

III.

1.

And therefore tell My people simple is the way -
That as, by doubting strangeness, they from Eden fell,
By doubting the familiar they from this must rise -
A portion of that presence that, being with Me, stands
Beyond the face that they most inward call their own -
Which they, by doubt made free, might from a distance see,
And make what was subjective their objective sight.

For they must stand apart from that which says, "I am" -
Which, so unseen, has made each sense and thought their own -
And be each one the Abrahams of their own mind -
Who leave their Babylons, and all their father's house,
And come into that land whose faith they now call doubt -
The breath in Adam breathed, "But I am what I am" -
That each thing seeming strange, so nothing might them bind.

2.

Yet each has clung himself to his own Babylon,
To be the king of that which he has called himself;
And let not moralizers say he would not be
A happy man could he forever so endure,
With ego as a god continuously to rule;
But woe to him that I alone can be that God,
To know a happiness and pleasure without bound!

For though his kingdom were a universe in size,
There yet would be a one who from beyond would have
A strength enough to cast him out and take his throne -
The Adversary who must always bring such pains
To each who reigns as god of his own Babylon,
That he, being waked, might humbly stand apart from self
And say, "How strange had been the throne on which I sat!"

"And strange be he who, spite of rite, has yet not seen
That faith in God be but that very self to doubt
Which is not measured by the depth of its own soul,
But always must be stronger than, or weaker than,
Those things with which he has identified himself,
That he who is the stronger must become their king,
And he the weaker but a dreamer or a slave!"

3.

Such is the mirror where strong and weak through each unfold,
That king and slave might in their cycles be as one -
Where he who strives to cast the king who cast him out,
Will, if he win, become that king whom he did hate -
The one who would then seek to cast him out once more;
Or letting kings him rule, by that submission make
Himself a power to crown far greater than which reigns.

Or where he who does not have faith enough to leave,
Nor strength of his own hate to win the throne he lost,
In plans and dreams makes worlds where he will think he wins -
Where silent judgment calls his weakness righteousness,
And thinks he would be king had he not been so good;
Or through those weaker yet will strive his loss to gain,
By making of himself their weaker or their pain.

Until in cycles love and hatred are as one,
And pain is pleasure without which he cannot live -
Which lets him judge the king, and makes him strong in hate;
And every peasant dreams that he has crowned the king,
Or that the crowd that cheers the hero cheers for him;
And none can think himself to be a slave, but loves,
And in himself becomes, that king he truly hates.

4.

So have I made this house, where each one seems a slave,
Amid a trillion worlds and trillion chances born,
To know but what of body, thought and will is seen -
Which once made dead, no cause nor chaos might remake -
Each dreams himself a king, with words and concepts crowned,
Who judging what he sees, and calling it his own,
By that same self unchose he, choosing, is enthroned.

And though he in that self but his own seeing knows,
None think it strange that it by chance so happen that
The things he thinks and how things are he calls the same;
Yet if he would but see his self likewise a thing -
With subject as an object so unfolded out,
That neither body thought, nor thought will, must compel -
He would, so doubting self, find truth within him rise.

5.

For he who, so being patient, seeks that happiness
That neither gods nor mind nor word of glory trusts,
But in its freedom finds more pleasure than in self,
Shall know himself as not, which as perspective sees -
A mirror of Me, who all, being infinite, is one,
That he, being infinitesimal, so be unique -
A one of endless nothings, endlessly being born.

Until from the perspective of that nothingness -
In houses clothed that each has shared and shall yet more -
He turns unto the land, and, turning, joins with Me,
That those potentials that from through that nothing rose
Might, in remembrance, through that nothing, now beyond,
Yet rise again, with parts and personality too -
A second Adam breathed, in gardens raised anew.

IV.

1.

And also tell My people where the way is found -
Upon the simplest, yet most difficult, of paths -
To doubt what seems to them the closest and most true -
The rightness of their selves, the wrongness of their foes,
The partial sight of each their judgments, wants and views -
That they who so remove all idols from the mind
Might see them each as but a one of all that might.

And, doubting, they must look on all they call themselves -
The breath in Adam breathed, within them breathed anew,
And all the permutations - body, thought and will -
Which round that breath, being seen, so weave in them "I am" -
That doubting those their own, they might their own selves see,
In that objective light, as ones of all that might,
And in their pilgrim spirals come near to My place.

For they shall so have brought the temple sacrifice -
To offer to the strange the first fruits of their flocks -
Which are the first because they come now to their minds -
And leave upon My altar that which thought them kings,
That, separate from those things they, turning, leave behind,
They see them in detail - potential as at first -
And in the fire of doubt those things, made strange, renew.

2.

Then shall they in each moment strengthen now the way
By that which within each experience so sees
With that same seeing from which the world at first arose -
Which, seeing every permutation of all things,
So sees that room that they experience now, and says,
"How strange the doors we chose, and strange the names we know!
How limited these things - but ones of all that might!"

For they who with awareness of that seeing look
On each the subtlest things that rise up to the mind,
And who, with Me as at the first, such detail see
As, making, knew, "How passing and so limited
Is this subjective sight - but one of all that might!,"
Are just by that so made a portion of that sight
Whose seeing is itself potentiality!

3.

And they who do not shrink from what that sight reveals,
Nor learn but by that sight, and not but by being taught,
Shall find no self but seeing, nor part nor whole their own,
Nor aught of them that lasts, nor is unshared by each;
But only that where now the is and not so meet
That choice, which as a mirror each will from was unfolds,
Might, separate from its pasts, the way within them call.

"Blessed are You, O strange our God, God of our fathers";
And by that prayer they doubt the worlds and self and thought,
That in their place a world and self to come might rise -
Where they no more that fruit of good and evil eat
That clothed the all within the houses of their selves,
And made them hate as evil what they wished were not,
And love as good those things that they would call their own.

For they who, so being separate, must have sacrificed,
Are by this deepest mystery of fate and grace
Become the blessed chosen by their very choice -
Who, standing back from that in which they once were clothed -
Where some things only, and not all things, seemed to be -
Are come into that garden where My love is known;
Until they fall again, in houses clothed once more.

4.

So they who know a servant must exist to see
Each house that, good or ill, unchanged or not, must be,
Shall fall to know a different house and history,
To their degree and kind of faith and sacrifice -
One not necessarily happier or so different,
But one, less bounded, knows, "How strange the house before!,"
And tests their faith that they might stand apart once more.

Until they give their lives, or have the greatest faith,
To be a portion of omniscience, joined with Me,
And know the greatest different senses and their worlds -
Where they will seem to do great miracles and signs -
As Abraham who, faithful, offered up his son,
Foretold the slavery that his children would endure;
And Moses, seeing wonders, knew them free at last.

There they will find those halls whose doors are yet unclosed -
Which leave, immortal, every house and house behind,
Foretelling that Messiah, always yet to come,
Who, standing past the worlds and greater worlds, proclaims,
"All time was as but doubt, that each, made strange, must pass,
And from each nothingness converge upon this end -
Which, all things so being past in so being strange, seems last!"

V.

1.

Then all whose seeing was doubt shall, seeing all things, shout,
"Blessed be His glorious name, which all these things contains!";
And, answering, I shall judge and, judging, seem to die,
That I whose rib, made free, this world, unstranged, made be,
Might from that world make free what there, made strange, knew Me;
And all that stood apart, that of Me shall be part,
Shall, as My son being born, with Me another rise!

For I who am the holiness beyond am made
From every smallest act of faith and sacrifice;
And as an exile who has left the all behind,
I shall be like a prophet singing from beyond
To that of Me that is the world about to end,
That in its Babylons She might not wholly die,
But by My love might be forever drawn to Me!

2.

And this shall be the song of songs that I shall sing -
"Come, for I alone am called, 'I am what I am' -
As there is not a thing that is the thing it is,
Nor thing that truly bears the essence of its name;
But inward in each part yet lesser parts infold,
And from each whole new wholes yet greater wholes compose,
That outward yet seek Me who always am beyond!

"For I am He who am not part of any thing -
Who, holy, separate, am unreachable beyond -
Unknowable who sees, but who cannot be seen -
As if I were a dazzling and a blinding light -
Who am a father born as if from My own rib -
Whose body is that form that always stands beyond,
And clothes within the seed of all potential things!"

3.

"And though no whole may reach what always waits beyond,
Nor yet its parts attain what likewise lies within,
Into that middle that we call experience -
Where We in spiral pathways enter and receive -
Both I beyond and You within bring each their lack,
That so the father and the mother make all things,
By which We, else unknown, are always yet complete!

"For as the human is not woman and not man,
But only known through that where they together join,
So know that middle whose beginnings are unknown -
Where I am caused by that which I have likewise caused -
A son become the father of His mother born -
Whose love for each is love that all things should exist
Within that nothingness where as a womb We meet!"

VI.

1.

And this the song of songs that I shall sing to Him -
"Yours is the presence of the strange that lies in Me,
Born outward in a form as wonderful as strange;
Yours is the same, yet mirror image, of Myself -
The purpose of that all that is My greatest form -
As Your beyond has yet been made from My within,

To be both Me and that which is My love's desire!
"Yours is the answer only known if We are joined,
Continuously begetting and being born in turn -
With You made greater, Me more equal, than before -
That what in Me is mystery in You is clear,
What clear is in You awesome in its majesty -
Where in Me those of faith are cast out and estranged,
In You their faith has made them portions of Ourself!

"For Yours are those who are, as You are, made beyond -
Who with Us now shall say, 'Let Us remake the world
From those potentialities of what has died,
But yet unsaved stood not apart to be as Us,
That but what is not Ours again shall be conceived -
Whose lesser worlds, being less, are, bounded less, more great -
As easier from that less it be to stand apart!'"

2.

"And endless are the greatest moments that shall pass -
With sons born lesser, though less bounded than before,
And ever easier, though yet worlds of less reward -
That ever newer Adversaries might yet bring
Those pains by which each thing might come to know the strange;
But never shall We reach the ending of our goal,
And always shall We lie upon this marriage bed!

"For as but in the infinite is order found -
As every other by a greater is surpassed,
But even chaos must eventually repeat
To make from its disorder patterns and a rule -
So endless is the love by which We save all things;
And yet unfinished is the joy that We now seek -
Ecstasy of which all is anticipation!"

3.

"And as the joy that comes from married bodies joined,
Such is the pleasure that from endless forms is born -
The ultimate of seeing from which all strangeness springs -
How being is, being loved, with presence so in-filled,
In all dimensions round, with none outside its bounds,
That its sole meant-to-be no deeper than can be,
And each that right-to-be must share as much as We!

"For as upon Our bed each thing shall join as Us,
So yet shall the resemblance of each thing appear
In Ours, the form-that-is-to-be, and in each thing
That there shares likewise that resemblance of Ourself;
And this must be the task of art and prophecy -
To speak that yet unknowable consistency
Of every thing, no matter seeming how unlike!"

VII.

1.

So write, Elijah, a book of that song of songs
Made of the scattered glimpses of each searching faith
That from the temple to all nations shall go forth -
Of those who from the desert prophesy Me one;
Of those philosophers who see potential forms;
Of those who preach Me three in one, and say by faith
I sacrificed My life and, doubting death, arose!

Of those who by the breath walk deathless by the way,
And call each opposite mysteriously one;
Of those who, mindful of their seeing, give up desire,
And know the strange of a nirvana yet beyond;
Of those who call that strange the I that looks upon
The body, thoughts and will that you have called yourself,
And selfsame looks on those that others call their own!

2.

As he who says, "How limited I am and small!,"
Speaks truth as much as I who say, "I am the great!,"
So though each truth that does not know itself as strange
Must by a greater truth be made to seem a lie,
Yet as in spirals that shall ever overlap,
That each must be, and yet not be, what once it was,
All evil shall be good, which draws Us to desire!

And though no self, being self, has known Me face to face,
Yet as in every symbol of each faith, once seen,
There is a form in which I shall Myself be clothed -
Though it be but to those who doubt that faith disclosed -
Write now a book whose parts consistent mirror the whole,
That when that whole those parts through each its middles sings,
So shall you find there this resemblance of all things!

Part Three

The voice Ezekiel heard from out the chariot:

I.

1.

My vessel is this one that goes yet does not move -
Which travels through all pathways yet is never turned -
This ship whose pilot is transported instantly
In all dimensions, and to every space and time,
That being still, he yet fills up the place of each,
To make himself identical with all that is,
And on the world his form and human image graft!

For by the mystery of this ship there is revealed
The meaning, not just function, of the human form -
Which in it bears all the dimensions of the world!;
And how each thing and what it is not be the same -
With is a strange to which beyond by doubt must fall,
And not a strange that it, made separate, yet becomes,
That each a mirror of each, in greater times be one!

2.

Here all the worlds that in the pilot lie within
Are now transported out, that they might stand beyond!;
And all that stand beyond, and are of all made strange,
Are now transported back, that they might lie within!;
Here all that lie within yet stand beyond the same,
Though not horizon-bound, from birth to death enclosed,
But outward here made in, their inward out unfolds!

Here is the mirror by which My greater love is known -
Where I am but each part, yet as each part am all,
And worlds rib-born bear Me, and by My saving fall!;
Here is the song of songs that makes My love desire -
Where beauty is here named a symmetry enmirrored -
The same, but opposite, in mind and form and seeing,
And man and woman clothed, in each the other's being!

Here is the complement where each its lack unfolds -
Where love from nothing all in each its place creates,
And each from each its own all that which it is not!;
Here all this world, though one, yet two-at-once must rise
In that same place where they the selfsame form each share -
Where every outward thing is but an inward born -
Which, mirrored by what it mirrors, its inward maker forms!

Here each thing is explained by that which it explains -
Where meaning is but that which its equation holds
When that which complements, and makes it one, unfolds!;
Here every outward of each house the balance bears
Of that community of minds contained within -
A balance that, unknown, shall at its end appear,
When all that which is hid shall at its last be clear!

3.

Then shall be seen that what My faithful dreamt is true -
That I a person made and act in history,
To work great signs, and speak the law from out the mount,
And as a king to judge the afterlife to come!;
And likewise seen that just as that which lies within
Must on the out be true, and share with it one form,
So by that outward world the inward mind is known!

For this house shares the form of that, which being within,
Shall yet unfold from the community of faiths
When at its end their balance shall proclaim Me Lord!;
And then there shall be seen a heaven without sin -
Where inward shall be out, as now but nature be,
That moral law become as natural law now is,
And none there might, though magic, ever more transgress!

4.

So shall this be the ship of which the prophets spoke -
That he who enters it upon the end of times
Shall show what love and all themselves cannot explain
Except by the configurations of a chance -
Why every house to mind is understandable -
Because its outward form is likewise found within,
And all its inward seeing but being there being hid!

For as each is a mirror of all that it is not,
So each that is as not, and as perspective sees,
Must as a seed infold that house where it seems born,
And, all its doors there mirrored, be through its life transformed!;
Until that seed at death no more reflection finds,
But now transported out another house unfolds -
The balance of that not whose fullness lies unknown!

And so what lies within must outward be reborn,
And from its outward fruit an inward strange remake,
That might that prior seed by its own doubting cure!;
And just as none can miss the child they once had been,
So selfhood is that continuity alone -
Remembrance of its priors in greater time recalled,
That, one with every self, the greatest house unfolds!

II.

1.

My vessel is that place from which all times have come -
Where I as man and woman from the garden fall,
And on the marriage bed the paradise complete;
Here in one place is both within and its beyond -
The seed within of all the world that might exist;
The nothingness beyond of all its rib and womb;
And in the middle doubt, which makes of choice their mirror.

For so the Adversary, doubting, first inquired,
"Must God remain beyond, and set apart from all,
And not within the world in every thing be known?;
And did the Lord not lie when He proclaimed His love,
To say that all things is the only thing that is,
And not that good or evil things might solely be,
Or that you might not have the knowledge of a self?"

And then the woman, doubting, asked of man the same,
"Is this at last not death, to have no certain form?;
And why should God as strangeness yet remain apart,
And not, admixed, familiar as each self be known? -
As how can He who is beyond the things that are
Be known, unless become a lesser, like our selves?;
And you a knower like Him, with pride estranged by doubt?"

She said, "This is the beginning of all histories -
That He who is beyond must so become within,
To be in every self familiar as your own;
And you from each beginning strive unto its end,
That through all good and evil, reaching for beyond,
You open up each door, each house and skin in turn,
And seem so to become what round your faith most fits!"

2.

I therefore said, "A stranger in the world you strive,
With sweat of brow so turning, once more to be Me,
In every house the mother in her pains must bear;
And when you close a door, she will but show a next;
Until, knowing all, the strange that now within lies mixed
Unfolds a new beyond - beyond what was beyond -
A strange that even from that strange has stood apart!

"Then shall you know that best resemblance into which
The histories of every lesser ship are joined -
Where, if all things exist, there also must exist
That place where all things are as much as in the whole;
And that place is as the unleavened bread from which
The leavened worlds arise, and into which they fold -
That place, now leaving, that by effort you must gain!"

III.

1.

The beginning is silence, and the silence speaks,
And clothes itself in words, in form and number told,
And in all other modes that endlessly unfold -
As for each some that might, there must a self that sees -
Which lives because it lives, and acts because it acts -
A being who must wake, and say in each, "I am,"
So bound to change and pain, and that which all must bring.

For silence is the seed, and words are but the fruit,
Of selves and worlds that in their certainty must grow
From out the balance of a justice yet unspoke -
A seed that, though but in an instant may exist,
Yet through a billion years, or seventy but, bears fruit -
That unremembered is that seed that was their cause,
As they be in their turn by their own fruits forgot.

And from each unpredestined choice of causes made,
Each animal and human, man and woman born,
So grows within the field of its own seeing bound -
Whose sensing makes him feel, and feeling makes him wish,
And wishing makes him think his self a cause undying -
That strange it seem being caused, or so being caused, so die,
Or silence bear those seeds whose fruit, being seen, says, "I."

2.

For he must be that servant portion of Myself
Who individually must bear each thing that is,
And every part perform that must in times be played,
That, playing, he no truth may in its meanings find,
But that he in each part that part as part must see -
Which each be some that might that, playing, so be he,
With all from first to last, and all he play between.

Until a billion eons, and yet more, have waked -
As must if all that might so through My ship unfolds
In histories and cosmologies without end -
From nothing, which at first in every place emerged,
To all things joined at last, in but one place converged -
Where love, which nothing loved, then all things loved, is done,
That it, none outward seeing, like nothing being, loves one!

3.

And as the worlds that join are but a sight being seen -
Whose seeing be but thoughts within the mind believed,
Of signals made whose light at last but nothing be -
So from but nothing, seen, the changeless has evolved -
As from a trillion places chance at last may rise,
And from a trillion chances cause and with it time -
Whose trillion times at last make worlds then lives then "I."

For as each place, being nothing, must as digits be -
Whose noughts and ones each touch, and touching so equate
Those numbers that lie hid with all the worlds they make -
To endlessness from nought, which are to them conformed
From simple to complex, as music, numbered, born -
So love be but a name, which all those numbers mirror -
Which most complex, being done, must simplest wake, being one!

4.

Then shall a trillion ages, being remembered, pass
As easily as a dream of sleep when night has gone;
And man, though changed, shall be that being who yet endues -
Who every world shall grasp, and every science learn,
And make, evolving yet, that place that always was -
A ship whose pilot goes, not but from place to place,
But, everywhere at once, fills mind and time and space!

So shall he be revealed as he who always was -
Whose rib of all his not is now to him restored
In skins that are as mirrors of those I formed at first -
With senses that are form, and wishing that is might -
That he who has, being all, the love to say, "Let be!,"
Might come into that feast where all, unleavened, meet,
And all My hosts, being joined, My paschal bread may eat!

IV.

1.

And at that feast the Adversary shall proclaim,
"I sing a greater tale than those of epic quests
Of heroes who from exile conquer or come home -
The infinite, which instantaneously occurs,
Unfolded as a tale in times without an end,
That so complexity, which only He can know,
Is made simplicity, at leisure to explore.

"And through this tale is now each death to birth retold,
That every healing of emotion might unfold -
When virtue has no more its taint of self-regard,
And even I am no more called, 'The evil one' -
Then we whose presence but to consciousness awoke,
To endlessness shall wake and, thoughtless plain, find home -
The ultimate that, counting, still yet be unknown."

2.

"So from that middle where the all and strange were mixed,
To make experience seem a world without beyond,
Let us each week count how His love has been restored -
How we whose faith was but a doubt of the unseen -
Who with our love believed that but some things must be,
And with our hate that all the rest should not exist -
Have by our doubt a new beyond and strangeness known!

"And diligently meditate now on that strange,
That constantly our efforts, turning to our doubt,
Might effortlessly their own concentration make -
Then we who count each tale that with that doubt must rise,
And know, with neither love nor hatred, 'So it is!',
Shall cast off evil, then too the pride of doing good,
And, doubting even doubt, be freed to the unseen!"

V.

1.

"Now on the first week count a tale of slavery,
And say how we built each our monuments to death,
That life, which has no certainty unless it ends,
Might by that certainty be cataloged complete!;
How, sleeping, good or bad, we shared that selfsame will -
That for our God or man, that self we chose be grand,
And death no more a strangeness, make for us a crown!

"Then shall we wake to know how we upraised that pride -
Enriched not by a source, but wearying the mind -
That in one image thought to bind our changing selves,
And so compel ourselves and others to belief!;
How we who had not walked those halls whose rooms are life,
Might, counting, doubt that house, where all our self being past,
We open up those doors that lead on from our last!"

2.

"Now on the second week count a tale of marvels,
And say how we remained the same familiar ones,
Though every mountain flowed, and all the seas came dry!;
How, sleeping, we, though moved, had yet not touched the real,
Nor stood apart to see our sense as but a sense,
Our thought as but a thought, belief as but belief -
Perceptions merely, wondrous they may be or not!

"Then shall we wake to know how, blinded by that dream
That constant in us played each moment unawares,
We named each nameless sense, and naming so recalled
Our long-familiar selves, and hid them from our sight!;
How we might, counting, doubt that self we called our own -
Which gave ourselves each names, of nameless causes made,
But might each other be, as what we, being, played!"

3.

"Now on the third week count a tale of wilderness,
And say how we for our familiar Egypts longed -
Where we, though slaves, no eye upon our selves endured,
But in our luxuries so dreamt we might remain!;
How, sleeping, we but planned each pain we would avoid,
Yet lived to see His love make all we loved to pass,
And all that, mirrored, we hate, by that same will, create!

"Then shall we wake to know how, clothing that desire
That, in a myriad forms, we valued as themselves,
We formed our ground of that which time must soon estrange!;
How we who, so being ruled by worry and by dream,
Might, counting, doubt those both that made us in our minds -
Which in our wrongness reigned, that wrong might seem as right,
And reasoned it so clear, that darkness was as light!"

4.

"Now on the fourth week count a tale of providence,
And say how we, though brought a paradise unearned -
Where manna effortlessly from the heavens fell -
Would yet not have our peace, but newer wants invent,
And problems in whose solving we might find content!;
How, sleeping, we once fell, yet would not fall to rise,
Lest eating so that selfless, we so selfless die!

"Then shall we wake to know how we might eat that fruit
That, taken without effort, tempts us to do right,
As once, as in a mirror, when tempted, we did not!;
How we might no more will nor outward cause sole blame,
Nor left nor right our worlds by opposites explain,
But, counting, hear those doubts that from the middle rise,
And show us our true thoughts when no more judgment lies!"

5.

"Now on the fifth week count a tale of rebellion,
And say how we would follow any who confirmed
That what we had become was what we always were,
And justified, by birthright, good and evil both!;
How, sleeping, we our strangeness so unconscious buried,
That we would never brave those kings we thought our slaves,
Nor, doubting ours their due, their friendless realms renew!

"Then shall we wake to know how, calming that offense
That in us, though being stayed, a greater tempting waits,
We lost that which by seeing, not by struggle, heals!;
How we who suffered, bound to every dying house,
Might, counting, doubt that will that in us willed desire -
Which had not wished for that which, separate from all pains,
Omniscient joying in love, and all its evil, reigns!"

6.

"Now on the sixth week count a tale of comforting,
And say how we through unforgiveness made of gold
That calf that from us banished all that child-like seeing
Which doubts that judgment that in pain was our delight!;
How, sleeping, seeming right, we would not that, beyond,
That, without selfhood, has compassion for all things,
Nor let our words, by seeing, to understanding deepen!

"Then shall we wake to know how, hardened by that pain
That taught us it was we, and not another, felt,
We all that was but might to our own suffering turned!;
How we might, counting, doubt what our impatience made -
Which with both praise and blame had built a fortress self
Impregnable to that first insight of our seeing -
That what we thought our self was not our truest being!"

7.

"Now on the seventh week count a tale of Sinai,
And say how we were born each thing made up of things,
That, so come from the mount, we fled that flaming sword
Whose fire had formed each one from His uncertainty!;
How, sleeping, we were parts whom other parts made whole,
That by that whole those parts were equal made our own,
And love of self and neighbor so become as one!

"Then shall we wake to know how we forsook that way
That, open to imagination, lets us change
Each permutation to that first before we chose,
And there so choose again, with selves and doors made new!;
How we who had not seen each whole as but its parts,
Might, counting, doubt those parts that made us as they rose,
And those which, those dissolved, our newer selves compose!"

VI.

And then the Adversary shall at last proclaim,
"Hear now the law that God Himself cannot withstand -
That love decrees that all, returned to the garden,
Must take again the fruit, and we take once more bread -
And man must fall again, and so unfold all things,
That he in cycles might a servant once more be,
And I to that division tempt him back anew!"

Then all the angel hosts shall in agreement cry,
"Is it not fitting that this one from whom came all,
With all its evil and its misery, should die?;
For justice is a mirror that whole and part makes one,
That he who causes harm must as those harmed be born;
And being is still that presence, always yet being filled -
Where here and now forever that which sees must dwell!"

But I shall say that none of them has spoke My will,
"Not one has understood this book who does not see
How two can be as one, and is can be is not,
And all and not all, both being right, might both be true! -
How so My exiles bear no blame of wickedness -
As it be right that I have made a covenant,
By which My judgment is no cycle, but a line!"

VII.

So build, Ezekiel, that house wherein the bread,
Once eaten, unconsumed shall stay before My face -
Where I am known a one alone without a peer
Of father or mother, of the beyond or love -
A king far vaster, yet much nearer, than the world;
For none is ultimate, but I who am the right -
Who made those it being right, which same I speak you now!

As he who calculates may wander without end,
But he who sees shall be, without an effort, true,
Build here that wondrous place, where no more mystery dwells -
Where all that which seemed strange is here a presence known,
Nor image rules nor guilt, though once they seemed My own,
But reason seen makes clear what simple I decree -
So selfless shall you act because no self you see!

Part Four

The voice that spoke to Zechariah in the land:

I.

My joy is the remembrance of those scattered booths
That now from Egypt and from exile are redeemed -
Those temporary dwellings that were each a place
Where space but seemed to be, yet could not long abide,
That in their autumns you might joyfully take leave
Of every house that in its permanence exists,
And with thanksgiving waves your loud hosannas cry!

So do not look upon the cities of the world -
Where all things must predestined by My love exist;
For no more shall the winter and its stillness come -
Where spaces without time might fill each frozen room;
But times without a space in harvest warmth must rise,
And at this last assembly not again depart,
That all might be as Me - from outward meanings free!

II.

1.

My joy is not the joy for which the worlds had sought
When yet the Adversary unrepentant ruled
That love that choiceless made all good and evil things,
With all their forms of father, mother and beyond;
But when the final day of the atonement ends,
Then he with all the hosts shall crown Me as the right,
And celebrate for once the festival of booths.

But though they cry, "Now have we truly known Your mind,
And permanently in Your cities shall abide,"
Yet I shall say, "Now shall your eyes behold a truth
That even you who saw the all cannot have dreamt;
For truth on truth must endlessly confound your sight,
That so your joy be multiplied in knowing that none
Is there who shares My mind, or whom I lend My name!"

2.

And I shall say, "Though the potentiality
Of all things must exist, yet too there must exist
Potential that the nothingness alone remain,
Or that but some things, or some other things, might be;
And there can be no certainty within these worlds
Of is, is not, of all or not, of one or two,
When contraries at once must equally be true.

"For within this uncertainty there is no truth
But one - that whatsoever there is that exists
Exists within that place that is reality -
Which is neither a subjective nor objective,
An infinite nor an infinitesimal,
A something nor a nothing, nor a space at all,
But that outside which is no being that might be found.

"And as this real is not but more than one alone,
So is its place one booth, unvarying and unmoved -
Whose outward decorations are the seeming change
Of contradictions sharing with each else in turn;
And all those changes, fruits of every Eden's fall,
Make from one booth what seems succession, booth to booth -
Where each, from first to last, must, each its own truth, pass."

3.

"And though that place does not bear always consciousness,
At some times it is knowledge, and perception too,
Experiencing that real that in its booths is found -
One soul alone that wakes the self of every seer -
Which sees the bodies, thoughts and wills now called your own,
And those that you before, or will again make yours,
Or that which shall be Me, and all that which I see.

"For there can be no other but that one alone,
That none should say, 'How small I am within this world!',
Nor, 'How within this universe impersonal
Has every rite and deed its magic and effect?';
But nature's vast is not more distant than the sense -
The clothings of that one that is the booth it sees -
Coincidence being prophecy made synchronous.

"And in that booth alone is there that absolute proof
To know that howsoever detailed science may seem,
And howsoever much an accident the mind,
The worlds are changeable, and not the one they clothe -
Whose space is as but time outfolded from himself,
And of himself sole knows he always was the real -
That, God or man, alone he must, not just might, be."

III.

1.

And therefore tell My people nearest is that one
Who on the mount said they should have no god but Me,
Nor make My image out of any outward thing -
That as, by Me remembered, they, being absent, fall,
By their remembering they, being present with Me, rise -
A portion of that joy where all in one place meet,
And all, remembered, is, though absent, yet complete.

For as, the world being vast, they from each meaning fall,
And earth and sun and God in each their turn displace,
So I do not exist, but inward am yet known,
When through My law, being done, they shall with Me be one -
Who on My Sabbath cease all that which brings no peace -
To murder, covet, steal, dishonor, cheat, lie, swear -
And with Me rest, being last - as all My booths be past.

2.

Within that last is this sole cause of paradise -
That there be neither space nor law outside the one
To make the seeming change from booth to future booth;
But only that which is the balance of oneself
Is cause to make the time or history that is next -
Both those where one might seem to work My miracles,
And those, like here, where laws seem so unchangeable.

And as there is no God who, mirrored, is not here -
Whose love, unlike that love that, seeing, was unmade,
Is not, unseeing, near, and from its clothes desires -
So one who knows but that he has not reached his joy
Must wish an opposite of that which he now sees -
The righteous that they might My kingdom's joy make real;
The lesser that they but a lesser pain might feel.

For none can plumb the balance of his true desire,
Or know, by merely thinking, that his wish be good;
But one by deeds must change what seems his outward world,
That more and more his will might inward be for Me;
And as each clothing makes from each its booth its next,
So too the booths of future times and histories
Shall by their better clothings bring My kingdom near.

3.

Then shall he know that last that must of all be best -
A joy that mirrors, opposing, that, which first, was worst -
As it, not prior wished, must, by none wished, be first -
An Adversary's hell, which fleeing, made all be -
As each beyond its pain, a lesser pain desires;
Until one reach that last, where will nor futures be,
And greatest joy no joy might greater than aspire.

For as what has been left must, as being left, be worse,
So less the suffering, more the joy, the futures hold,
That none resenting should by hate or want desire
To re-experience or re-enter what was past;
But he who no more dreams of outward what but seems -
Though meantime he yet deems he in that house yet dreams -
Shall come to greater goods yet closer to My joy.

4.

And he who in his moment ceases from desire,
With every hate and want that moved time back and forth,
To know that still that therefore has no future time,
And, wishing no more joy, must therefore be true joy,
Shall no more ask, Who is Messiah whom we seek?;
But each might be the anointed one who brings the last,
And by his lonely choice attains My Sabbath joy!

For he who, though not perfect, knows the Sabbath day,
By being still that last and truest Sabbath knows;
And though his wish, being partial, leaves that day behind,
Yet on that partial day he shall be joined with those
Who on their Sabbaths gazed on tribes and temples both,
And to that weekly turned, when time was as but done,
In that same last booth being, with all who rest were one!

IV.

1.

And also tell My people how that one is found -
Upon the nearest, yet most hidden, of all paths -
To, as they see, remember, not just, seeing, see,
Nor live but in the now, nor by experience be -
That they who so see worlds, and know they shall not last,
Might that which is to come, remembered, make yet past,
And that which, past, they mourn, remembered, make reborn.

For they who know My voice must speak to them alone -
Who hear the oral law, which never put to pen,
Proves inward sense abides, and inward prayer must rise,
Though billions who so willed seem outward unfulfilled -
Shall prize but their own seeing, and not but what be seen,
That harm be no more out, but inward to be found,
And, grasping not, know heaven, though they in hell be bound.

2.

Then shall they find My law, which nothing outward bids -
Which in them knows, "You are yourselves the latest ones,
With all dependent on the choice that you now make,
Though all around you see those equal with yourselves,
Contemporaneous in that space He says is not" -
And by that they are crowned, anointed at the last,
Though some perceive the king as one already past.

For as a sleeper dreams a last before a first,
That what already was seems but just then to be,
And things but recent past as ancient truths long gone,
So there does not exist a thing outside oneself
To say what they recall might be not that foretold,
Nor those they outward see what once and shall yet be,
Nor time have but one past, one future nor one last.

3.

Until that sleeper wakes, and by his waking saves,
Though there be but the one in different clothings garbed,
And not a remnant of a self at last endures;
But as none wish to stay that one that they now are,
And even kings grow tired of what they wished to be,
So when that sleeper wakes, not one shall be displeased
Within that place wherein desire can find no lack.

For though none should inquire as to the age or change,
Or the identity, of that which shall be saved,
The presence of each yet shall at the last endure -
As that which is desire, which does not wish to leave,
Must know those things to which it does not wish return;
And that is My remembrance, bringing times to end -
The mirror of that potential which those times began!

4.

And so the trumpet of atonement always blows,
That he who is the sleeper once again might wake
To dwell one final time within his summer booths,
Before the world that through its place so melting flowed
Extends itself once more into its winter home;
Until the cycles at the last assembly end,
And one by choice forever dwells within My booth!

For so the mirrored visions of Myself agree -
The booths like that unleavened bread that has no space,
And leavens out between each change from booth to booth,
That so desire might modify those frozen worlds -
Where cities without will, being wishless, once seemed still;
Until the Adversary's words no more have force,
And one by choice at last shall clearly hear My voice!

V.

1.

Then all who were remembered shall, remembering, shout,
"Hear, O Israel, this last our God, being last, is one!";
And I shall bind that one upon their heads and hands,
And on the fringes of their clothes, and on their gates,
That at their rising up, and at their going down,
And in the midst of every of their thoughts and dreams
They might remember that which, past all time, is still!

For though there is but one who wholly seeks the truth,
Yet they might wish, in part, to leave behind the false,
And cling unto a stillness past the flow of time;
Until remembrance, to which they constantly turn,
Becomes the ever-stiller spirit of the last -
Whose meditation compensates for every loss,
That they might wish no more re-entry to the past!

And though the only truth they know be physical -
To bind that last as best as possible to things -
Yet every Sabbath to a fuller Sabbath leads;
Until that future, ever anticipated
As ever unreachable, in joy is attained;
And on that Sabbath they shall seven circles take -
Which three mirrored three, and one, My best resemblance make!

2.

And all shall in remembrance in those circles join;
For My salvation else could never be complete -
As harvests owe the land as much the laborer,
Who in a poor society would not be rich;
And bounded are the evils any might commit -
Which being paid with yet a million deaths or more,
The worst might at the table with their victims eat!

And as My people to My symbols bind themselves,
So are the nations bound to Israel as their priests -
Who are a still around which they in circles wave,
That they who seek My blessing show that gratitude
Which is the precondition of the joy they seek -
To realize what they forever have escaped,
Who follow My commandments tenfold to that place!

And there in symbols of the mind they shall perceive
Themselves as each three branches in one branch conjoined,
With each a form of that desire that made the world -
The ancients by Tiresias the sage being led,
The easterns by a Buddha so compassionate,
The westerns by a Christ now risen and alive -
That they with Israel, My fruit, four species, cry!

VI.

1.

"O save us who desired that all things should exist! -
Who, seeing good and evil, wished its opposite -
The poor, unsatisfied, that they might be as gods,
The gods that guiltless they might be the ones below;
Or that an earth of pleasure be an earth of pain -
Where tragedy is not entirely unwished
To bring the downfall and the blindness of a king!

"And bless us who know, like Tiresias, the source
Of every form of man and woman, son and wife -
How, sole on time's ladder, self-enjoying, self-condemned,
We never found, in being, a state of permanence,
Nor glory nor disgrace that would not fade away;
But in our leaving every thing in turn behind
We caused all things inevitably to arise!

"And lift us up who like that sage now choose Your joy,
Though yet the sphinx speak his too-love-enriddled mind -
How, causeless, forms must be, yet, formless, be but cause -
Whose chances endless past must all things make at last -
That what the times uprear Your timeless cities mirror!;
How choice could have no power to end the flow of time,
With all the good and evil we must yet endure!

"Then shall we thank You who have made us for Your name!;
For formless is that love that nothing formed may bind,
To say all must yet be, or what that all decree -
That love might be not must, but that which choice but might -
Whose doors potential seemed, being endless, Your own like;
Or if our pasts be endless then we must have been
Already all those things that love says must exist!"

2.

"O save us who desired a holiness beyond! -
Who, seeing all things end, wished for its opposite -
The strange that is the mirror of all it left behind -
As all was but the mirror of it that was to come -
That so desire be love of self unfolded out -
Which, being aroused, makes each the other more themselves,
Causing, more than generation does, attraction!

"And bless us who know, like this Buddha, that true cause
How this, though non-existent, balance of our mind
Yet from abstraction might its own potentials make -
How beings by faith might, just as much by love, arise,
And all the worlds be but the clothings of desire,
Though earths be made with cause and karma camouflaged,
That science and biology seem in themselves!

"And lift us up who like that monk now choose Your still,
Though yet the tempter speak his too-despairing mind -
How happiness on strangest things is always based,
Of tastes and body parts, and pleasures of the mind,
And even those that, greatest, must too come to end!;
How suffering is that which cannot be overcome -
As that which can is but a challenge, not the pain!

"Then shall we thank You who have healed us with Your name!;
For from the mirror of our selves Your triumph comes -
That as all our desire is but fulfillment mirrored -
Which proves that we shall see what mirrored shall more yet be -
So You by Your own love more God are and more great -
Who by our faults here mirrored, more perfect are more praised,
And we, so loved, by love our more remembrance make!"

3.

"O save us who desired the certainty of right! -
Who, seeing the vessel, wished for its opposite -
The man and woman that the cycles might so end,
And in their place a one unchanging standard raised
By which we judged the worlds that we had left behind,
To pardon all confusion, pain and ugliness,
With all the rest that as a king we once condemned!

"And bless us who know, like this Christ, the inward peace
That comes to those who by their lowliness are made
Unceasing vessels of new insights from above -
How we who no more made our minds than made ourselves,
Being blamed not for our thoughts, but only what we grasped,
Might, emptied and made equal with each else, wish more
That there be one who sees than that the one be us!

"And lift us up who like that son now choose Your life,
Though yet the serpent speak his too-discerning mind -
How all the things that might no tale but might may tell,
And each those things, being things, no thing but being prove!;
How we as in a desert but that sameness know -
Where judgment, good or bad, might be to none ascribed,
That, fasting on that plain, yet none may humbled rise!

"Then shall we thank You who have called us by Your name!;
For we but now have understood that mystery
That words can outline, but may never comprehend -
Whose truth You always patient, seeming cruel, make wait -
That one who, good and bad, is yet their seer alike,
Might, willless for reward, nor heaven knowing exists,
Yet give himself in trust that, You being just, it must!"

VII.

I.

Dwell, Zechariah, in that harvest booth of joy -
Where there is neither space nor time, but both are one -
A sleeper who arises to that waking dream
When finally the bread is mixed with wine in joy,
That by their combination laughter fills the heavens;
And if but tales of man and animal combined
Aroused such laughs, so shall your humor be the more!

For I who said to Abram, Now I know your faith!,
All-knowing yet have waited this, the final choice,
That all the circles now complete, a seventh day;
And this and this alone is ultimate meaning -
Not a thought, nor an ideal, nor a purpose,
But a place that needs no more justification,
When none can question it, not wishing to depart!

2.

As the world, full of subtleties, is infinite,
But, once known, by a letter may be symbolized,
So join with those who in their joy dance with My book –
Not this whose order speaks a mind that does but dream,
In chaos where unknown is every future thing;
But that, in meanings steeped, and in all numbers clothed,
Renews itself in each, wherever it unfold!

And as this world remembered shall in absence find
A presence, as was being, but as the nothing like –
A unity uncaused, unthing, unmight, undying –
So here where all that was seems but a question asked,
Awaiting him who shall the final answer speak,
Say now those four that are the letters of My name,
And out of that ineffable so make Me one!

www.ingramcontent.com/pod-product-compliance
Lightning Source LLC
Chambersburg PA
CBHW060431050426
42449CB00009B/2247